I0410062

Coloring Time

Animals, Mermaids & Dragons

Created and published by S.Klösges, Mönchengladbach Germany, 2018

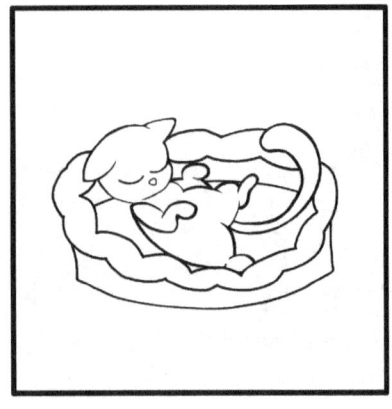

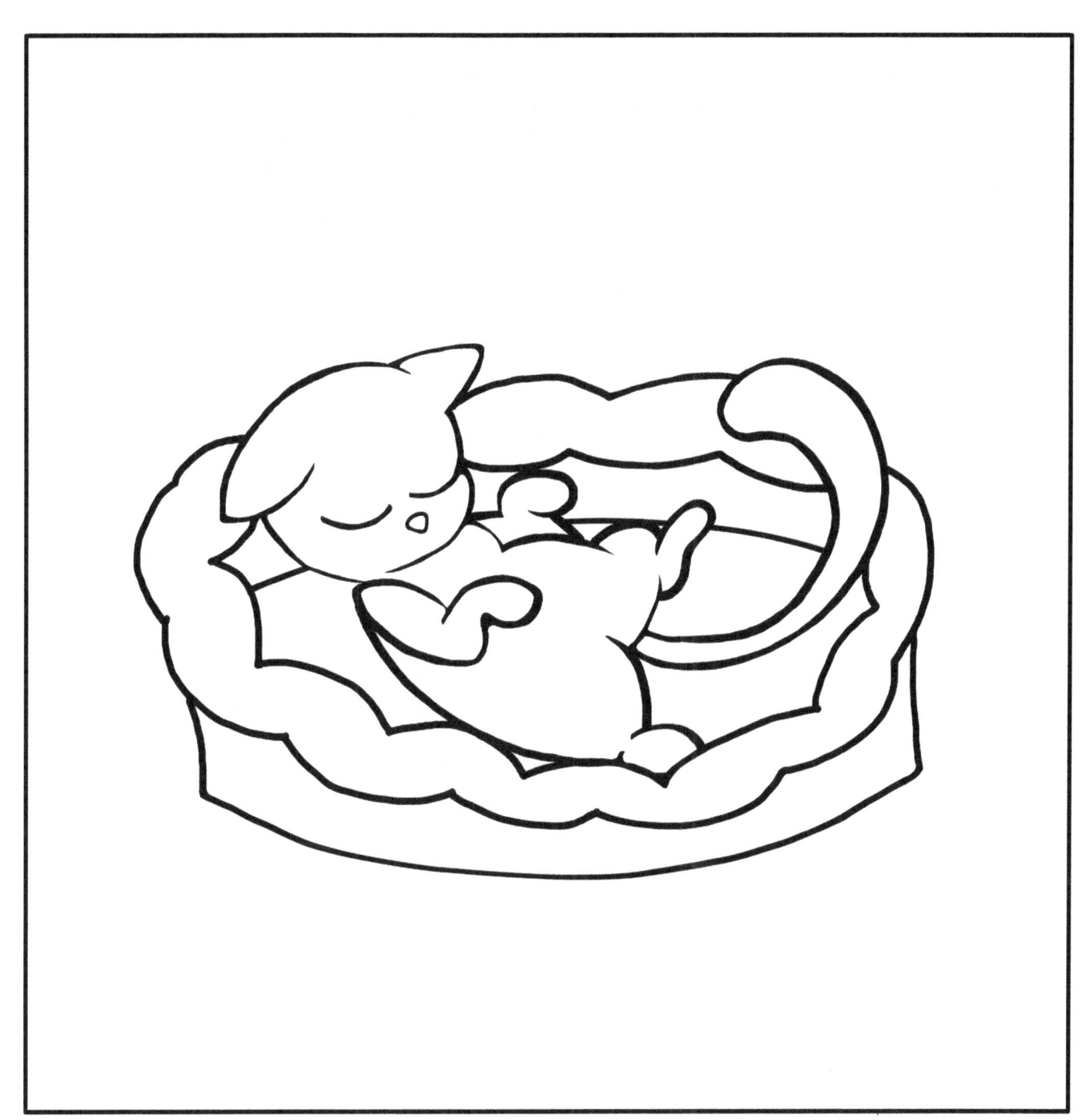

Sie haben Fragen oder Anregungen? Kontaktieren sie uns:
meplayitonline.com | info@meplayitonline.com

www.ingramcontent.com/pod-product-compliance
Lightning Source LLC
Chambersburg PA
CBHW080834310526
45788CB00020B/3558